ALL MY LOVE FOR YOU

POETRY

SANA ABDULLAH

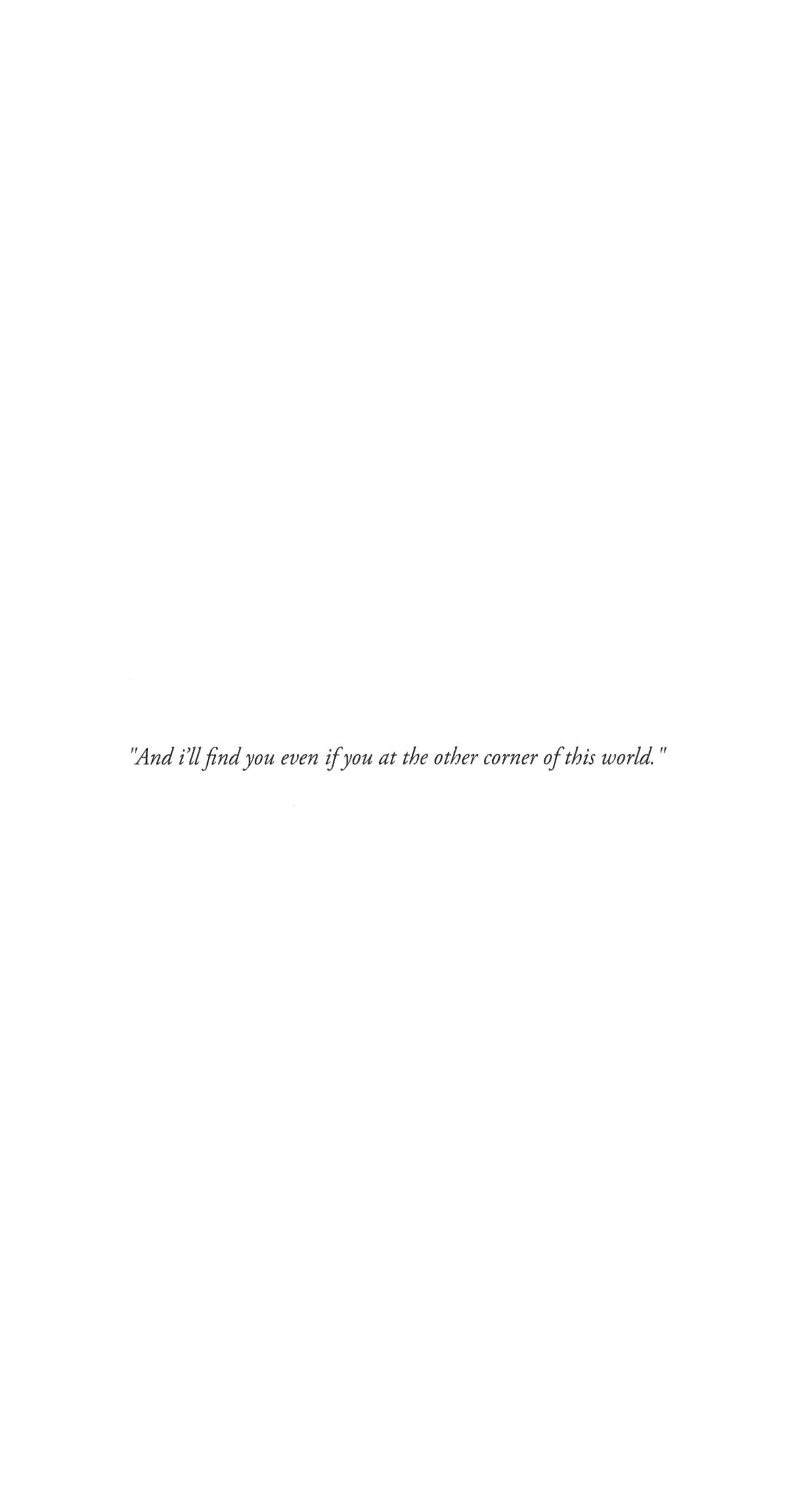

"And i'll find you even if you at the other corner of this world."

Contents

Acknowledgements   *vii*

Prologue   *ix*

1. You   1

2. Comfort   3

3. Distance   6

4. What Do You See When You Look In The Mirror?   7

5. The Nights   9

6. Streets   10

7. Its You   11

8. My Man   13

9. Safe Space   16

10. Love   18

Acknowledgements

aksjwfdhweifhwejwoidjwpeodkp okay i still can't process what i am doing but yea i wanna thank all the people in my life for motivating me and appreciating my talent.

Prologue

all my love for you, maybe these words aren't enough to tell you what you mean to me. But here i am just trying to make you smile because that very thing is my absolute happiness.

1. YOU

I am just in love
With the flowers out there
With the smile you wear.
With the biting thorns
With the way you moan.

With the candy clouds
With your presence in the crowd.
With the beaming sunrise
With the brightness in your eyes.
With the famous wine
With the way you shine.
With the stairs to climb
With your honesty in crime.
With the start to decline
With your beautiful neckline.
With the soul that sparkle
With the thought to cuddle.

2. COMFORT

It was disappearing
fading, slowly
And its gone now
The pain.
You made it go away
As soon as you took me in your arms
And looked me with your starry eyes
it was different before
all the nights filled with cries

my world just stopped for a second
how beautiful everything was in that very moment
and then you just laid down
holding my hand
as if that was the only thing
you wanted on this land
You made me glow
Only by a glance
and i knew that
you just changed all my plans
so i slept a peaceful night
just to wake up next to you
made my heart jump
and all my feels right
how i spent every moment
being loved by you
how beautiful you made my life

you fucking have no clue
and i watched the sun rays
piercing your skin
as if i was jealous of
how it was touching that thing.
it was you
what i needed to survive
hunger was some lost thing
you were my only bribe.
All the days i spent with you
Saw all your scars and all your hues
It wasn't enough

i definitely needed more of you
"Don't fucking forget me" thats what i said
"you are the only thing I remember" you tilted your head
resting it on my shoulder
It was good to know
that you were gonna miss me
and I didn't know how to hide
All those tears
So you just wiped them and
and kissed me

3. DISTANCE

We are miles apart
But somehow still connected
You are my other half
But unfortunately still seperated
I wanna hug you tight
And close my eyes
I wanna feel your warmth
And your beautiful smile
May this distance come
To an end soon
i need you to complete me
Exactly like our moons

4. WHAT DO YOU SEE WHEN YOU LOOK IN THE MIRROR?

They ask me what do i see
when i look in the mirror?
Well the thing is its not me
its a person very dreamy
What i see is him
Not in actual sense tho
But i do see his
hands in mine

how he shines
when he smile
how beautiful we look
side by side
The mirror opens a gate for me
a gate that leads to only him
All my pains go dim
by just a small grin
I see him fixing his hair
or sometimes his
fingers tangled in mine
his beautiful deep brown eyes
and him kissing my neckline
Well in short
All i see is you
It might be crazy to a few
But my soul recognizes only you
and my heart and my eyes too!

5. THE NIGHTS

In the nights when i fail to see the light
I hope you'll show me the path
The path i was always scared of
The path that haunted my soul
The path i never wanted to see
The path of love and glee.

6. STREETS

I'll build you a house
With the things you never saw
I'll give you the emotions
That you failed to show
I'll give my heart to you
So that yours isn't alone
I'll walk you home
On the streets we've grown

7. ITS YOU

I wanna be in your arms
Till the night goes off
The sun sets down
And the wind is cold
I wanna feel you
In my veins
Your hands wrapped around my neck
Like a golden chain
wouldn't it be beautiful
To dance in the rain
keeping each other

like photos in the frame
You are the sun to my moon
You light up my world
like a morning
in the middle of June

8. MY MAN

I don't ask for a lot
But oh god!
If I ever fall in love again
I want it to be with this man
He makes me feel wanted
and understands me
even when I'm muted.
The man with whom
i want all my days to end

and who is also
my best friend.
He makes me forget
all my worries
and his beautiful eyes
hide so many mysteries.
I'm well aware of
our differences
and yet somehow he manages
to conceal my miseries.
His voice is no less than cocain
i want to keep him
as close as my favorite chain
And if I ever fall in love again
I want it to be with this very man.
If someday
he asks me to prove love
I'll willing give up my every breath
coz he's the only human
i want to love till death.
Everything's bearable
when I know he's there
And him walking away from me
is honestly my worst nightmare.
In a crowd of hundreds
he's the one I'll search for
he healed my wounds
i don't think i feel them anymore.
I know our efforts

won't go in vain
neither do i care
if the world calls me insane
Because if I ever fall in love again
I want it to be with this man.

9. SAFE SPACE

I wanna create a safe space
for the people who crave
absolute and unconditional love
where they don't have to behave
As per the rules of society
And can enslave
Their true emotions
And nobody's gonna
judge their actions.
I wanna create a safe space
For the people who were traumatized
by their very own families
who are scared of the memories

Of their childhood
because all they would see
Is pain and tears and scars
I wanna create a safe space
For the people who were betrayed
by their close ones
be it their lovers
Or friends or even cousins
and their wounds still bleed
Because healing needs
Love and patience and support
I wanna create a safe space
For everyone and every race

10. LOVE

Love is the path
Through which we get to know
Whom actually we are
It let us know what we actually feel
It let us know how we deal
Sometimes
With some people it play games
But still its the most beautiful feeling
Falling for all is not love
Falling for none is not done
The day you will choose your one

Will be the day
You will get into heaven